a day without fear

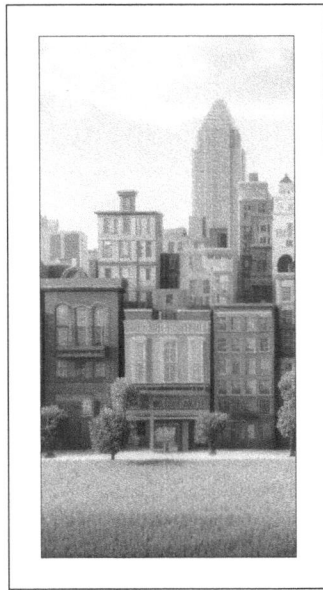

a day without fear

david james

poems

SHANTI ARTS PUBLISHING

BRUNSWICK, MAINE

A Day without Fear

Published by Shanti Arts Publishing

Interior and cover design by Shanti Arts Designs

Shanti Arts LLC
193 Hillside Road
Brunswick, Maine 04011
shantiarts.com

Cover image by Rawpixel.com / AI /
1393880530 / stock.adobe.com

Printed in the United States of America

ISBN: 978-1-962082-74-7 (softcover)

Library of Congress Control Number: 2025941652

For all those who have gone before,
and all those who are still on the journey,
spreading love, kindness, and hope.

CONTENTS

ACKNOWLEDGMENTS

Bluestem: "One of Those Days

Bookends Review: "A Thin, Ragged Piece"

Bourgeon: "Our Pandemic Blues"

California Quarterly: "The Art of Sinking into Love"

Chest Journal: "In Ways We Never"

Chiron Review: "When I'm Gone"

Dunes Review: "The Blame of Autumn"

Escape into Life: "How to Become an Existentialist"

Gyroscope Review: "A Shrug of the Shoulders"

Homestead Review: "The Day Will Come"

Hurricane Review: "After Finding Out My Friend Has Been Sleeping with Another Woman"

Iconoclast: "Holding Happiness"

Immortal Verses: "Either/Or"

Iodine Poetry Journal: "There is No Comeback"

Mississippi Crow: "Picture Postcards"

Plainsongs: "The Truth Shall Set"

Poetry East: "What Happens When the Sun Comes Out in Mid-January"

Poetry Explosion Newsletter: "The Fall of Another"

Poets Speaking on Poets: "Ten Days After Russell Edson Died"

Rabble Review: "The Need for Poetry"

Rockhurst Review: "On Not Understanding the World"

Slant: "A Couple Dozen Springs"; "Praying to My Whatever God"

Sub-Lit: "What's Your Problem"

Uppagus: "Beyond All This"; "That Old Sad Story, You Know the One"

Verbal Art: "To the Disease That Will Kill Me"

Wild Violet: "The Poem in My"

"Get Some Masking Tape" originally appeared in a chapbook, *I Will Peel This Mask Off*, March Street Press.

I

"Have no fear of perfection—
you'll never reach it."

—Salvadore Dali

A COUPLE DOZEN SPRINGS

Tonight at midnight
                                        spring
saunters into town wearing shorts and flip-flops,
rings on all her fingers,
a bright T-shirt that reads, "Stop Blaming Me
        For Your Problems." It's raining
in her heart of hearts. It's flooding
behind her eyes. She points at a tree
        and buds pop out. When she steps
on a lawn, a green flame arcs from her footprint like spilt milk.
                I have twenty or thirty
springs left,
if I take care of myself, if it's written in the stars that way.
I'm waiting for the apple blossoms,
        for the lilacs to bust up, for the bulbs
                we planted on a mid-winter's day
to show themselves,
                        though I doubt they will.

The first spring day
                                        shakes the last
        quarter-inch of snow
                out of my body.
                In every tree,
birds remember how to sing.
The world stretches, yawns,
        licks her lips with possibility.
                                Though it's a long shot,
I'm hoping
                        she'll kiss *me*.

DEAR AUDIENCE

—for Billy Collins

I love every one of you, really.
You're my new best friends.
My last set of best friends
were a bit slow on the uptake,
missing my immense insight and humor,
but I can tell you're smarter,
more enlightened,
true devotees to art.
I know if I ramble too long
on the origin of a poem,
you'll find it mesmerizing.
If I stumble over a line or two,
or mispronounce a word,
it will be endearing to you.
If I mix up my metaphors
here or there, you'll forgive me
and claim I did it for 'effect.'

But enough small talk. It's time.
It's time to break open my heart
and spill blood like words
into the air, as if there was a way
to save you,
or me,
or anything.

OUR PANDEMIC BLUES

my friend Jack tells me about
this new syndrome called 'surge depletion.'

it's like
our human batteries are running low after working so hard to stay
in place due to COVID, economic collapse, an election
that resembles a circus with albino bears riding bikes
through town, promising to give us a piece

of the pie,
lying out of every orifice possible. it's all i can do
to get out of bed. i'm in a capture-and-release
program but never released. i'm a kite in the sky
with no strings. i'm a yellow mask without a face.

what's a sane
person to do? grin and bear it? eat more gummies?
camp out for hours in front of a computer and embrace
your digital self? it's our first pandemic, people. we shouldn't blame
ourselves for surge depletion or ambiguous loss.

i say wake up,
drink some tea, watch the sun crack open an autumn sky.
hell, buy yourself some down time and forget about the cost.

BEYOND ALL THIS

One tree rises in the center of the field
with a man up on a branch, swinging his feet

back and forth, toward heaven, toward earth,
as undecided as the rest of us.

Lost among lunches, babysitters, work,
he tries to find a place where he doesn't

have to *do* something, *be* somewhere, *listen* to someone.
He wants to sit where the wind sits

to rest her weary voice, where the days hang out
telling old stories, where the nights go to drink beer

and tap their feet to live music.
He wants a place of his own where he can

set his head on straight once and for all
and walk with a strange faith, if nothing else,

in the human desire to add up
to something beyond human.

WHAT YOU GET USED TO

As we sat outside last Tuesday,
the sun sinking through maples and birds calling out
a young hawk on the telephone pole,
a falling star got caught up
in our apple tree.
Its loose ends were tangled
in the top branches,
and as the star tugged to break free,
apples rained down below.

We'd seen this before and knew
the star would die if we ignored it.
So I climbed up with lawn clippers
and a saw, snipping the knotted ends,
cutting branches when I had to.
It didn't take long
before the star pulled away.
He thanked us with our own light show
and then shot back into the sky.

The hawk flew away, followed by
four or five sparrows nipping at his tail.
You picked up the apples
for the compost bin and then
we sat down to drink iced tea and watch
the sun finally dip below the treeline.

All in all,
it was a pretty typical day for us.

AFTER THIRTY

"No man is a pessimist after thirty." —Goethe

Goethe was dead
wrong on this one.
After thirty, you look around
and see just how much
you *haven't* done,
how life didn't turn the way
you wanted it to,
and you're left to wonder
how you'll ever get back on track.
Now your legs ache
after running and playing football.
Muscles you never knew you had
flare up and throb.
After thirty, I'd say pessimism
sets in the way your hair
thins and recedes,
gradual, almost imperceptible.

If you're strong willed enough,
you ignore it and get on
with your life.
If not,
you end up a walking stiff,
and every color appears black to you,
every mistake a declaration.
You resign yourself to living out
a dull, battered existence until,
with the flick of your wrist,
you'd sell your soul
to the devil

and think nothing of it.

ON NOT UNDERSTANDING THE WORLD

My yard is an ocean of leaves.
I'm sure there's a metaphor
I'm missing in that.

Blue sky, sun, forty degrees
and the maple tears apart, two days yet
from being completely bare. Yellow pours
down like crisp hands of butter. It's done
with a flare to announce the end
of fall, the promise of winter, that whore,
who comes for revenge, tit for tat,
as if we had any power over the seasons.

She'll barge in, that one drunken aunt
who spills wine on the carpet, drops her plate
of food and laughs until she's numb.
She wants to break open and pretend
the world's fine, even though she can't
figure out what this life is meant to be.

Let the trees die; let the snow bury us as always.
Somewhere beneath it all, a seed takes root, plants
itself and dreams of spring.   And waits.

TEN DAYS AFTER RUSSELL EDSON DIED

who died on April 29, 2014

An ape walks down the street, dragging his intestines behind him. They leave wet streak marks on the sidewalk.

Someone stops him to say, "Do you know your innards are trailing behind you?"

"Why, yes, thank you," the ape says. "It's really no different than you carrying your severed head in your hands."

Someone's head looks up from his hands to his neck. "I never thought of it that way," says someone. "It's like Charlie who carries his left kidney in his pocket."

"Or JoAnn who has both of her breasts in plastic bags in her purse," replies the ape.

"Or my brother-in-law who wears his first failed marriage all over his face."

"Hell," says the ape, "I once saw a person pull his entire childhood in wagons and boxes behind him."

"That's sad," says someone, turning his head into his stomach to cry. The ape sees this, puts his huge hand on someone's shoulder and pats it.

This moment, this little conversation, this touching between someone and the ape, will be something they both remember for years to come.

TO THE DISEASE THAT WILL KILL ME

I'd rather not meet you.
Go bother someone else,
preferably a terrorist or criminal,
a psychopath, a child murderer.
Let there be some poetic justice
in our screwed-up world.

If you have to find me,
and I know you do, make it quick, please,
that's all I ask.
Of course, I'd want a little time
to say my goodbyes, kiss my lovely wife and children,
kiss my grandkids and family.
But not too much time—
I'd start regretting and getting pissed off
and resentful and I wouldn't be able
to savor my final days alive on earth.

Maybe three weeks? A month?
I've never died before so I'm not sure how much time
I'll need to say what I must,
kiss who I want,
pack my spiritual bags for this next journey.

I'm looking forward to it though:
I've heard it's relaxing and quiet
with tons of alone time.

AS THE ECONOMY DIES

Twenty-three tomato plants, ten peppers, green beans
and three cucumbers. Fire lettuce, the size of melons.

Thirteen basil plants for my wife's homemade pesto. Two zucchini
to supply the neighborhood. This year, I've gone green,

constructing raised garden beds out of cedar planks.
They're victory gardens, though nothing's been won

and much more has been lost in this quiet town:
jobs, houses, more jobs. A few marriages have been squandered,

spiraling down the proverbial drain. Still, the sun
rises each morning and shines equally on the blessed and
    the blank,

on the gifted, on the cursed. We can walk with our heads down
or lift our worried faces up to the moving sky.
    Thunder and lightning

crash around us, bringing rainwater for the garden
where plants grow and climb, bush out and blossom.

With luck, I'll pick vegetables this summer, bite hard and
    give thanks.

BIRTH OF A PLAY

The playwright locks himself in his room, for drama's sake.
He knows this play will not come easily. It's been burning
under his skin for years, elusive yet obvious in so many ways.

He undresses, puts extra towels on the bed and lies down
on his back, legs apart. The ideas are coming in one-minute
intervals. He trembles and shakes, his skin on fire. For
hours, he writhes and screams; he bites his pillow; he
sweats and pushes until deep into the night when the play
is born. It's a frail, bloody mass, but he holds it against his
sweat-dried chest and sings to it. Rocks it. Stares into its
face and sees himself, his mother and father, sees what he
must have began as.

His heart sinks when he realizes how far he has come
to know
so little.

FOUND: DEAD

I found a dead bird in the bird bath.

Out of respect, no other birds were flying in
to drink or bathe. Did he die naturally?
Did he commit suicide, taken over by wrath,
heart broken by a slutty bird wife?

> I walked to the shed, grabbed a shovel to begin
> the digging. Buried him in the garden
> with no words of praise or sorrow.
> I have my own problems.

May you find peace, bird, in a wind-filled afterlife.

IN DENIAL

Every year I chop down the Rose of Sharon, chest high,
and by mid-summer, it's twelve feet tall.
In full bloom, it's one massive beehive
with a few hummingbirds thrown in. Soft as a baby's thigh,
          the petals rain down
into a magenta carpet. A heat bug's engine call
drones from some unknown tree, trailing off into silence.

I miss my grandchildren, both of them sweating through a Japanese
summer. Like a down-and-out heroin addict fighting withdrawal,
I suffer through time and distance, trying to survive
without their hugs and smiles, without the silly nonsense
songs, without the kisses goodnight. Like the rose,
my petals are dropping slowly, the years lost in wind
and nightfall.   I feel this sense

of urgency, but deny the truth. I want the day to freeze
in slow motion; I want my children to shrink back in time, pose
again in their empty rooms. I want to lose this extra weight and
wake up with a head full of red hair. I want to plant a Rose of Sharon
from seed, water it, watch it rise up and grow.

But time says no. She drags me forward, heartless, on a whim.

PRAYING TO MY WHATEVER GOD

Forgive my face
my hands
my spit on the sidewalk
Every thought
burrows its tiny little tunnel
into my heart
Each desire
floats up to the top
of my eyes
and begs
for life
I turn my head
and every path
looks the same
the one and only
the mundane
the manicured
There are so many ways
to go
How can anyone
start off without panic
without hair turning
gray and falling out
without wrinkles
without a scar
across the heart that says
    You know absolutely
       nothing
    You have no idea
      what you're doing
So you kneel at the base of
trees the moon the stars
Your face bends up
toward the sky

and you pray to whatever it is
that breathes life
into your arms
that breathes
darkness into the air
that breathes
forgiveness into your
one good ear
saying your name
over and over
for none of the other gods
to hear

HOW TO BECOME AN EXISTENTIALIST

Maybe we're looking for something
that's not there, that's never been there.

We see a shape of the clouds or a blazing sunset or a leaf
falling into our lap, and we imagine it has special meaning,

that the world would make sense if we knew the code.
What if there is no code? What if spring

is just spring, a thunderstorm, only rain?
What if there is no grand design, no holy grail,

but billions of random chances and choices in every moment?
Instead of pondering my future, worrying about my purpose,

I should relish eating this apple, sing
when I feel like it, carry you up to the bedroom

to make love. I should close my eyes and listen to the birds,
live in the minute and take nothing for granted—

this cigar and iced tea, the hawk flying overhead,
holding a small rabbit as two starlings nip at his beautiful wings.

ONE OF THOSE DAYS

After ten years of cleaning my pool,

I fell into the water today, fully clothed.
One foot off balance, the sudden recognition, an "Oh fuck" or two,
and into the ice cold water—shoes, pants, shirt, wallet—
everything soaked. This morning, I also broke my wife's favorite
teapot, the Brown Sadler from England. Tried to glue
it back together but that was hopeless. I'm snakebit.
Cursed. Stuck in a force field of rotten luck, going down

with no parachute, free falling toward evening.
Some days rub you raw, and there's nothing you can do.
Your life is a sentence and you're the proper noun.
No matter what you try, you're the person, place or thing
sitting on the tracks with a southbound train coming fast.
It's practice for the end, a couple of decades from now,
God willing. We all end up wet, broken, cursing into an empty room,

our last breath unable to bend a single blade of grass.

A CURSE FOR THE WOMAN
WHO FIRED ME FOR NO REASON

—my very last poem on this subject

In your eye socket,
I'll plant a hundred maggots
just to see what happens.
Your hip I'll use
in my garden like a gargoyle,
driving away rabbits
and the occasional deer.
Your hands get ground
into a fine soil,
sprinkled into the tomato bushes.
Your arm and leg bones
I'll use as stakes for the green
beans, peas, as markers
for two rows of carrots.
And your heart, black and useless,
I'll set out
as dinner and breakfast
for the old crow.
He'll smell you for miles
and come flapping, landing
to stare at the steaming mass.
In his own time, he'll peck
and try you out, think twice
about eating but eat anyway.

From the telephone poles, tree tops,
from the peak of an old barn on Lahring,
your heart
will be shit out
and finally worthy of its place
in the world.

WHEN I'M GONE

Remember me, love,
when it rains,
not for the obvious metaphor,
but for the grilled cheese sandwiches
and tomato soup,
an afternoon movie,
that one train
barreling through town.

PICTURE POSTCARDS

My toes turn beige, then orange, and then crumble off inside my shoes. Every October, I stagger around like a new drunk, convinced my life is over and done with. My hair falls out, circling in a V formation above me, before flying south. My skin dries up, becoming off-yellow, and my fingers and hands crash to the ground like fleshy apples, fodder for the late night deer.

Another year slips out the back door without a goodbye or a wave, leaving me to stare out the windows as the world collapses into picture postcards. It would help if I grew in wisdom or knowledge, but I simply know less than I did a year ago, and I'm more certain of that.

As the afternoon carries pieces of me out under the night sky, this string of breath I hold frays a bit, pulling me forward, though all I want to do is go back.

THE TRUTH SHALL SET

This man grabs his truth
by the tail and drags it through the mud and rain
before
hanging it on the antique telephone booth
in his spare room, stolen
from a 7-11 store outside Ft. Wayne.

Another guy keeps his truth in his back
pocket,
rarely bringing it out into plain
view. From her tenth floor penthouse, the woman
mixes and drinks the truth as she stumbles in her low-cut black
evening gown for no one to see.

The single
mom of four sells her truth for a two-room shack
at the end of a dirt road south of Lincoln.

A shape-shifter at best, the truth can be
whatever you want—a law, an excuse, a reason,
a lie.
You grab it, hold it close to your heart and let it lead
you where you want to go, or where you've already been.

SEPTEMBER AGAIN

Across the road,
where the path weaves a slow walk
to the old swing,
five sheep graze,
puffs a shade darker
than the field.
Small blackbirds perch on their backs,
up for a free ride, pecking
through wool.

It's September
and I stare at the willow leaves
floating down, thin, yellow.
They appear out of nowhere,
suddenly catching the eye,
twirling it to the ground.

And winter will come just as fast—
one glance and it'll be here,
everything gray and white
and then spring
and then summer.
The trees take the brunt of it all,
shedding, freezing, blossoming.

We step to the window
to see where we're at, which season,
which life, and the sheep are gone.
The trees rock out there, emptying themselves,
the branches moving together
in the wind like lips.
They are saying one thing:
this   can't   go   on   forever.

AFTER FINDING OUT MY FRIEND HAS
BEEN SLEEPING WITH ANOTHER WOMAN

Two hearts for twenty-five years
become one heart

                                 here

and one heart   there.

One of the hearts is breaking,
cracking down the middle,
spilling out old memories.
The other
crumbles and falls,
pieces shattering across
the kitchen floor.
The air is thick with blood and excuses,
with regrets and reasons and doubts,
bleeding for what was
and for what wasn't.

One heart sits alone at the table,
rubbing its shoulders, rocking lightly,
unable to sleep.
The other curses and tries to drink
itself out of being a heart
and into a handful of raw meat.

Across 800 miles,
the sadness travels
back and forth
from one heart to the other,
beating
like a truth
no one
wants.

WHAT'S YOUR PROBLEM?

It's not that I don't care,
it's that I don't give a fuck.
There's a difference in intensity.
Take abortion. Take the death penalty. Take stem cells.
I don't give a fuck.
Let women do what they want;
let criminals get what they deserve;
let scientists work to cure diseases. Whatever.
I have my own problems.

Life falls from the skies and I'm trying to pick it up,
grab what I can, eat what won't kill me in the end.
If you choose to dedicate your life to work
and money and prestige, I don't give a fuck.
If you die for a cause or religion or to screw
your ex-girlfriend, I don't give a fuck.
If you starve yourself, drink until your liver
squeezes out your navel, carry grudges on your
sinking shoulders, I really don't give a fuck.
We're all given the exact same day down here
to breathe and eat and live. The existentialists
got one thing right: you become what you do,
nothing more, nothing less.

So if you decide to hunker down, sulk, hold your regrets
in both hands like diamonds, I don't give a fuck.
I'm going to smile as the sun blazes down after
four days of hard rain and flooding, sip this delicious cup
of coffee and marvel at the few clouds left tumbling
through the sky today.
The only person I'll give a fuck to is my wife, my love,
which I know brings me joy,
and sometimes, her too.

AS TIME GOES ON

As each year came and went,
the man noticed the tree
outside, the one in back,
how its bark shed
like fur, how it bent
and swayed in time to the wind.

He remembered how his dog tracked
in his last dirt before being found dead.
The man buried him, like the others, religiously.

With each year, something pinned
itself to the inside of his heart,
which he imagined was not red
anymore, but bruised and mildly
dry, an item to be stacked
on a shelf or a cart.

The years began to rain down,
one suddenly became three.
The man looked up into the black
sky. And then a strange thought in his head
fell, like his entire world, into the swollen ground.

THE BLAME OF AUTUMN

Two gray horses
stand outside the shade
of an enormous elm tree,
early fall surfacing
in their manes.
There are no other trees
in the field, only decaying stumps,
fallen hulks, soft, broken legs.

The horses follow their mouths
from one fence to the other,
chewing, shaking away the last wave
of deer flies. Under the sky,
the horizon trees darken
with the hint of evening.

This is when autumn crawls out
of the shiny coats of horses,
and climbs up the tree to kiss each leaf.
Of course, the leaves blush
and begin jumping free.
The wind promises to carry them anywhere
except back.

The two horses lie down,
sleeping through the reign of leaves,
dreaming themselves south of snow,
out of the cold winds,
out of their large
and guilty bodies.

THE DAY WILL COME

my poem stopped, looked me
straight in the eye and spit.
i figured this day would come,
though it surprised me at the end of october,
leaves everywhere, clouds looking like gray tits
about to rain. every other tree, even the plum,
was a gnarled skeleton. two yards over, a dog barked.

who the hell are you, the poem said,
to bring me into this dying world?
i'd rather be in the stomach of a shark,
or one of the millions of red
leaves composting into grass. i had no response,
like always. i don't know what i'm doing.

two decades from now, my kids will sprinkle
my ashes into lake huron and then go to lunch
with who's left of the family. my soul, canoeing
in the stars or threading up through the roots
of a tree, won't give a damn about poems.
like leaves, the poems will fall, break down under the snow
into rich dirt.   finally, there will be truth.

A LITTLE MORNING PRAYER

Let me doubt my ability to give up
when times seem hard, question
whether I need to question
and accept that moment of grace
      the way the sky offers itself
      to the sun
      each day
      without fear.

II

"Always do what you are afraid to do."

—Ralph Waldo Emerson

THE POEM IN MY

The poem in my knee can predict rain

coming, but not whether it's a storm
or steady drizzle. The poem
in my ear hears that train
in the distance long before

it's close to Linden Road. On a warm

spring day, like today, the poem in my eyes
can tell the future. It's not always right,
but it has its moments. When I'm torn,
conflicted, unable to decide what to do,

the poem in my heart tries

to speak. Its voice is wet and garbled.
Sometimes, I forget it's there
and go about my business, a simple guy
hoping for more luck than anyone deserves.

And the poem in my skull
is the loudest. It shouts into the night sky
like it's dying, which it is. Those poems
bleeding out, strange and beautiful,

are the ones, I admit, I refuse to write.

GIVE AND TAKE

if you give me that smile
that lights up the house,
that one that takes me back
to being a newlywed, amazed
at my good fortune,
I'll convince the sun to join our family.

if you give me that look
with your dark eyes
that sends hope through my bones,
into my heart, I'll get the flowers
to bloom at your touch.

if you give me your laugh
to let me know we'll walk through every drought,
every crash, every fire, every moment
that makes us doubt the existence of God,
I'll invite the moon over for dinner.

and if you give me your hand
when I'm falling and can't see a reason
not to give up and hit bottom,
I'll gather a thousand stars
in our back yard and you can make all the wishes
you want
or need
to be happy.

CARRY THE CROSS

"I am poured out like water; all my bones are out of joint;
my heart within my breast is melting wax." —Psalm 22:14

Your cross is my cross.
I hear it dragging on the ground behind me,
feel its steady weight on my shoulders,
slowing me down.
Each year, it becomes more visible,
                              more real.
On this day,
you walked into darkness,
your heart flaming with faith,
and lit a path toward heaven.

I do my best, lugging this wood,
giving up, forgetting, finding my bearings,
starting down the road again.
It's difficult work, Lord, as you know.
And most of the world refuses to believe—
they drop their crosses and step into
oblivion; the end becomes nothing more
than a cold brick wall, a wet hole in the earth.

Help me, Lord, to hold my cross
with two good hands and drag it through the city streets
up to the place of skulls.
Let me work and sweat; let me stretch my arms out
when the time comes; let my eyes stare up
into the night sky.
Be the light I see;
be the faces at my side;
be the voice I hear
after my heart
melts.

THE ABSURD CURE

*"This is the eternal problem if ever there was one;
for living means alienation."* —Eugene Ionesco

From my island, I see your island.
And I can see you, wind in your hair, sitting under a palm tree,
sand sifting through your fingers.   I wave.   You wave.
If the wind is right, I can hear you yelling to me, and vice versa.
We do our best as refugees,
making a home, pretending this is normal, brave-
ly closing our eyes at night to fall
into another darkness.
It's a miracle
we have the desire to stand in the morning,
dress, eat, work, without slamming a fist through the wall,
without screaming our lungs dry. Two seagulls

glide across the red sky as a new day
rises out of the sea. I call and wave to you,
but you're asleep, lost to me,   as usual.
Still, I dig my feet in the sand. Keep waving. Pray.

THAT OLD SAD STORY, YOU KNOW THE ONE

He had a table as a hat, a sofa as a shirt.
He wore a TV as pants and his shoes
were white buckets. When he talked,
his voice sounded like a cat buried in dirt.

His house was a large red wagon
set up on blocks. In the yard, he grew bamboo,
opium, vases, tiny horses and a gene pool.
His neighbor complained but stopped after the man
gave him a new dresser and shared his pay-per-view.

The man worked at the local ice cream shop
and gave away his salary to support a mule
known for laying large eggs.
He used to be married to a woman
who dressed in appliances with two footstools
as shoes, but they divorced after the lawnmower died.
He was born premature, on his last leg,
with a near empty tank. They tried their best
but their son couldn't pull through. The two grew apart.
The man tore up his sofa; the wife blew like a powder keg.
To this day, they both dream of a red lawnmower
cutting clean lines across the yard and wake up depressed.

Sometimes life throws you a handful of bent nails
or a blow dryer that doesn't work.
Sometimes you close your eyes and try to get through the rest
of the day like you belong somewhere. Anywhere.

FREE WILL

If God was a bird
he'd be a sparrow,
pecking away
in the back yard, heard
every dawn

as he wakes us from our narrow
grave of sleep.
When we look at him
out the window,
he winks, flies away.

A THIN, RAGGED PIECE

Let's say you're on your last thin string
of hope   your kids are hungry
you've lost
your minimum wage job with no benefits

your 2006 Chevy needs a new muffler
two rear tires   an o-ring
for the oil
leak and your left wisdom tooth aches like hell

Your string of hope   frayed and a little wet
is in your pocket one early spring
morning
as the sun rises on the first robin you see

Let's say you smile   Let's say you feel
the face of the world slowly turning toward you
so you
warm your hands on a cup of tea and begin to sing

EITHER/OR

No matter what you do, who you know,
how big your car is, how much money
in the bank, time takes you by the short hairs
and swings you around like some wet dough
until you break apart and fly

into a hundred bite-sized pieces. Today, it's sunny;
tomorrow, thunderstorms. The very next day
the world could shrink into one last breath
as your heart says, "That's enough," and you drop to your knees,
unable to utter your final goodbyes.

There's joy, love, grief and pain. Each of us pays
for every ounce of happiness, every tear of sorrow.
You can settle on regret and limp away into the darkness,
or you can smile at this chance, pray
for more time as you gaze up into the immense sky.

A SHRUG OF THE SHOULDERS

No wren's in sight, no bluebirds.

Five birdhouses and no takers so far.
It's early, April 21st, and it snowed this morning.

I cut the tulips and daffodils yesterday before the freeze came.
Every year, spring arrives, acting like a petulant tzar
waving her hands, cursing everything

in her path. Her hormones
bounce up and down, careening off tree
trunks, burrowing across fresh lawns.
Sometimes the sun shows itself for an afternoon, on loan

from the summer, but it's unreliable. We're ready
for the warm weather, the picnics and lemonade,
the baseball games, the hammock, that ice cold beer
in a lounge chair by the pool. Any wise man or woman

will tell you there's a price to be paid
for good fortune. With all your might, you can try to steer
your fate into calm waters, but no one

can predict when the winds will change, when the storms will
rise up, when that next hurricane will lift its ugly head

over the horizon.

DEAR GRACE

On a crowded street,
how will I recognize you?
Is there some special hat
I should look for? A twinkle
in the eye? Wings protruding
from your jacket?
I've asked for you nearly everyday
of my adult life
to settle upon my children and
family like some invisible dust
that won't wash away:
Send your grace, dear Lord,
to be with us though we are not deserving.
Is that you in the apple tree,
calling like a bird to me?
Are you in this fleshy smell
of cut grass? Are you dissolved
in a glass of wine, stretching out
inside me as I drink?

I'm sure you've visited
from time to time—
there is a certain contentment
I can't explain,
times when the world goes right
for no reason, when the sky lights up
and I understand the shaking ground
beneath my feet.
I hope to meet you, dear grace,
at least once before the end,
face to face.
I'll raise my glass to you,
smile, say a few inadequate words of praise,

and together we'll watch the full moon
crawl across the heavens.
Your long stories about God
will finally make sense.

IN WAYS WE NEVER

—for Margo, August 22, 2011

A friend of mine dies at sixty-eight, two weeks
after a diagnosis of cancer. That's the way
I want to go—quickly, but with enough time
to say my goodbyes, to stare into the eyes
of those I love, to hold them against my cheek

and taste the salt from their tears,
have them taste mine.
Love won't repair the wound, but it's the prize
at the end, the answer in wet clay
that we shape into a loving and sincere

heart.   The dead stick to us
in ways we never imagined—a hawk in the sky,
a cup of steaming tea, a scene from one of Monet's
paintings. Their bodies and faces, almost divine,
settle inside like a clear dust.

I love Borges' idea that we don't die until the last
person with a memory of us passes away.
My friend, you're here, lodged in the cells of my mind.
My grandparents, cousins, aunts and uncles, they fly
like kites in my red sky, glowing like ash.

THE FALL OF ANOTHER

"autumn hanging on by a thread . . . " —Eugenio De Andrade

It's more like twine or rope tied to a sturdy tree branch,
the noose around autumn's bare neck

squeezing the last few breaths out of his lungs.
It's an occupational hazard. Every year, it's the same story:

autumn rides in on a blaze of color, but starts cashing bad checks
for whiskey, women and cocaine until he's strung

out and wanted in forty states. It's the coward's way
before the prison of winter sets in and everyone's slate is
    wiped clean.

He struggles a bit at the end. Then stillness. He hangs in the yard,
a limp rag. As the north wind blows, we watch his warm
    body sway.

PEOPLE CHANGE

—after Franz Kafka

If I was a huge cockroach
lying in the dark in my room

and you were my true love,
my dream, my purpose,

would you open the door, broom
in one hand, violin in the other,

and love me no matter what?
For better or worse? Richer or poorer?

Human or insect? Or would you jab me
hard in the butt

to see if I was alive or dead?
Would you wish I'd leave quietly

during the night and disappear
into memory, someone caught

in photographs, someone to be grieved
and missed? Things happen. People change.

As I crawl up the wall
and hang from the ceiling fan, my heart bleeds

for you and only you. I'm just saying,
I'd break my shell and let you have it. That's all.

THERE IS NO COMEBACK

—for Debbie

"I don't like your new poems," she said.

"They're depressing. All about death and shit.
What happened to the funny ones
you used to write?" I don't have a good
comeback. Maybe it's a way to spit
in the face of the inevitable, to outrun
what we know is coming in the end.
The longer I live, the easier it is
to imagine digging my own hole in the earth,
to imagine the utter darkness I pretend
or hope will not be there. We all walk into the abyss
sooner or later. And anyway, a poet can't lie
to himself for long. Life and death are two sides
of the same old coin that keeps flipping in the air.

Maybe it's my feeble attempt at saying goodbye.

THE NEED FOR POETRY

A poem walks into a bar and orders
your full attention—your body, your mind,
every last nerve left under your skin.
The poem demands that you stare at it
with both eyes, your hands tied behind
your back, your feet stuck in wet cement.

Sure, you can read a novel at a baseball game
or listen to one while driving to Toledo.
You can read two pages here and then seven pages
next week. With a play, it's the same—
you can watch it on youtube while the kids scream
and fight at your feet; you can read "No Exit"
a page a day for ninety days.

But with a poem, you must kneel at the altar
of living. You must be willing to jump into the pit
with someone else's demons, or open your brain
with pliers to examine your bias and belief.
You must stare at your naked body for hours,
recall your forgotten memories in color,
catalog and describe every wish, every grief,
every joy and fear, every failure and love.

The best poems slip inside your body
and live there, gently reminding you that others
have feelings, too, that you are not always right,
that the world spins everyone like a top with absolutely no
                                        guarantees.

GET SOME MASKING TAPE

for you alone
I will peel this
mask off
my face strip
by strip
releasing the
real me
but
there's a mask
under that one
so I tear
it apart
and there's another
now I rip
at my face gouging
and scraping
mask after mask
one face after
another
until I'm left
with a brain
balanced
at the tip
of my spinal cord
all this
I will do for you
but face it
this is not
what
you
want

EPILOGUE

—for my father

Your days are numbered
and we know it.

With such a damaged heart, you've lived longer
than anyone imagined. The doctors
rarely see your type, and these are their words,
alive by sheer stubborn will.

You're pulled through the day by a hunger
for living. Everything is done at full-bore
or it's not worth doing. You've outwit
       death and his red pill
       by laughing in his face,
raiding the hell out of the cookie drawer,
eating seconds of apple pie, refusing to admit
there's anything wrong with butter.

At this point, you're alive by the grace
of God and some mysterious blessing.
But when that day comes and your heart quits,
tossing in the towel at the far end of fear,
the idea of you will go on—there once was a man who wore
his joy in his heart and wasn't afraid to sing.

DECEPTION

January 3rd and winter has come and gone.
Empty trees, brown grass, a few piles of snow

left to melt. Two days in a row the sun
has graced our sky. The eternally hopeful have begun
to plan for spring—starting seed pots, tilling

backyard gardens. Us old-timers smile, know
the heavens will bury the world in ice

and a foot or two of snow before next week's end.
When your guard's down, you get hit, a roundhouse blow
nailing you face first into the mat.

Winter sits alone with a bottle of Jim Beam, a slice
of lemon and nowhere to go, no one to go to.

She won't hit rock bottom until mid-April,
at best. Only then, after we've paid the full price,
will she stand, brush herself off, leave us to our own devices.

THE INVENTION OF JOY

It's nothing you can buy or sell,
though people try—through sex or drugs,

cars, cottages, whiskey, tattoos.
Remember that one guy whose foot missed the mark and fell

down the side of a cliff, climbing to find
joy. Or your cousin who dug

her own grave with a handgun pointed at her heart.
There's no end to what people will do—

have affairs, steal watches, make rugs.
It's best to think of joy as a blind

fish, driving an old golf cart.
You'll know it when you see it

and there's no telling when it'll come
or go, or why. If you're lucky, joy parks

on your front lawn, calls your name, and life is fine.

WHAT HAPPENS WHEN THE SUN
COMES OUT IN MID-JANUARY

The first sun
in ten days shines
into my skin
and makes me want to dance like someone
in love
for the very last time.

Let's make this day count.
Let's pocket it
like a brand new dime
blazing on the sidewalk.

If I could, I'd mount
the clouds and sail
through the blue wind up there.
I'd hunt
for God and the angels,
for the pearly gates, the holy grail.

In this sun, I'd wash the feet
of all the dead,
happily pulling out the rusty nails
one by one.

HOLDING HAPPINESS

Happiness comes and goes like a hummingbird,

here one second, gone the next, even though experts say
the tiny bird shouldn't be able to fly at all.
Some wags spend their time and money courting the absurd
notion that happiness is a place, a destination,

an island within reach, you know, a certain and easy haul
from shore. But anyone with two cents worth of brains
knows that's dead wrong—happiness is a fog
that rises, disappears, smothers. It falls
on you when you least expect it.

It melts if you grab it; it crumbles like a dry log
in a bonfire. Happiness floats in the cool air
and sometimes you breathe it in, other times it blows
through your hair. One day, it's in the cheap corn dog

you buy; the next minute you're standing alone at the corner,
    undone.

THE END OF THE WORLD?

—for Debbie

Room 8, a vag bleeder,
Room 3, a two-year old
with a fever of 104,
Room 6, a man with seven nails
pounded into his left foot.
It's another busy night in ER
and we've never seen this one before.
"How did this happen?" the nurse asks.
"I did it myself," he says. "It was an accident."

Seven nails stuck clear through
his foot, but snipped on the bottom
so the nails are flush to his skin.
Not much blood, really.
The doctor carefully removes
each nail, dabbing holes
with alcohol.
We give the man
a tetanus shot,
wrap his foot with gauze and tape,
provide complimentary Tylenol
for pain, though he refuses it.

He limps out
of the emergency room.
We watch him for awhile
hobble down the street,
and realize, like all the others,
even if this guy
was Christ himself,
we'd never believe it.

THE ART OF SINKING INTO LOVE

There's more to love than holding

onto each other's heart—there are cups of tea in the evening,
doing laundry, making lunch, sitting in the back yard

as our grandson figures out how much of the world
he can grab in his little hands. There's the porch swing,
the barbeque, pool, shopping, the hard

forgiveness. Love sinks through the skin
into the bones, the cells, the DNA.
Our lives wrap around each moment
and we begin to believe we can win

any battle, shape and mold any gray
into blues and reds, yellows and greens.
All roads lead toward hope.
On the worst of days, love gives us the answer

to the most difficult question we've ever seen.
So here we are, on the downslope,
walking toward the great fall,

but I'm not scared. I'm not worried.
Arm in arm, we'll guide each other

into that final dark squall.

Born and raised on the third coast, Michigan, DAVID JAMES has published eight books and has had more than thirty of his one-act plays produced in the United States, Ireland, and England. After working for forty-five years in higher education, he retired in 2022.

SHANTI ARTS

NATURE ▪ ART ▪ SPIRIT

Please visit us online
to browse our entire book catalog,
including poetry collections and fiction,
books on travel, nature, healing, art,
photography, and more.

Also take a look at our highly regarded art
and literary journal, *Still Point Arts Quarterly*,
which may be downloaded for free.

www.shantiarts.com

www.ingramcontent.com/pod-product-compliance
Lightning Source LLC
Chambersburg PA
CBHW070012100426
42741CB00012B/3205